Library of Congress No. 2006922450
Graziano, Claudia. Meerkat's Safari / Written by Claudia Graziano; Illustrated by Michelle Barbera.
A Meerkat's Adventures Book.

Summary: A plucky meerkat leads young readers on safari through the African plains.

ISBN: 0-9778072-0-7

SAN: 850-2862

Meerkat's SAFARI

By Claudia Graziano

Illustrated by Michelle Barbera

Inspired by Daniel Sweeney

A MEERKAT'S ADVENTURES BOOK

www.meerkatsadventures.com

Dedicated to the animals of the world

Pack your bags
and grab your hat.

Let's go on safari!
Follow me, the meerkat.

I'll take you to places
where animals run free.

Listen for clues
and guess who we might see.

This gentle beast peeks over treetops with ease.

Can you guess who likes to nibble on leaves?

Giraffes

When giraffes are thirsty
they bend down low.

Eighteen feet tall
giraffes sometimes grow.

They close their noses
to keep out dust and sand.

Giraffes live in herds
and sleep while they stand.

Out on the plains this king is hard to miss.

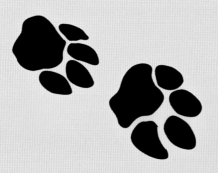
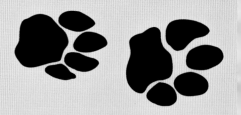

What kind of cat would rather roar than hiss?

Lions

Lions are fierce
and big and strong.

They hunt at night,
then sleep all day long.

Lions see in the dark
with eyes that glow.

Two lions rub cheeks
to say "Hello!"

This creature glides and slides on its tail.

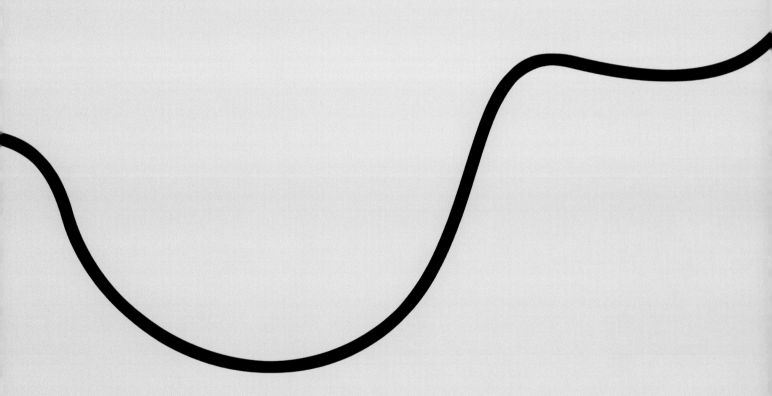

Can you guess who, instead of fur, has scales?

Snakes

Snakes can crawl,
coil, climb, and swim.

Several times a year
snakes shed their skin.

Some snakes are short,
some as long as a bus.

Some snakes have fangs
but not all are poisonous.

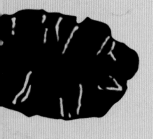

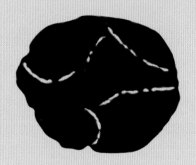

This fellow has ears that flap in the breeze.

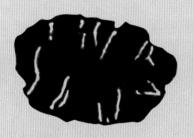

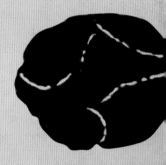

Who do you think sounds a trumpet with a sneeze?

Elephants

Elephants are
the largest mammals on land.

Their noses, called trunks,
they use like a hand.

Elephants can live
to be 60 years old.

Elephants get stomach aches
when the weather is cold.

Not a parrot, a peacock, or a chickadee…

What feathered friend has webbed feet and pink knees?

Flamingos

Flamingos are known
for their long skinny legs.

In nests of mud
they lay a single white egg.

Flamingos live near
salty marshes and seas.

They mingle in groups
called colonies.

Try to guess this one, its name is the key:

Who do you suppose is more like you than me?

Monkeys

Monkeys are noisy
and playful and fun.

They like to eat fruit
and snooze in the sun.

Monkeys can swing
from tree to tree.

They use their long tails
for balance, you see.

This neighbor calls out with a snort and a bray.

Can you tell me who tends to blend with the shade?

Zebras

Zebras have stripes
so they can easily hide.

Lions and leopards
they watch for, wide-eyed.

Zebras, like horses,
love to eat grass.

They're feisty and wild
and run very fast.

Congratulations!

Our safari is done.
You've guessed all my friends
and met every one.

Until our next adventure,
it's time for me to go.

Take a trip to the zoo,
there are more animals to know.